UNDANCEABLE

MERRILL GILFILLAN

UNDANCEABLE

FLOOD EDITIONS CHICAGO 2005

CONTENTS

UNDANCEABLE

SOLOMON SOLSTICE

Sunrise more
a porridge than a fire:
low slough

of off-whites, cold grays.
One long lone rosy bar
far south—

Antarctic pudding
unfolding nicely to
pale peony

flush and shoal. Step out,
have your picture
taken with a star.

The Solomon north fork
a perfect solstice flow:
Gaunt December nonchalant,

a scattering of trees,
the palette bleached
to the master tones:

Distant cornstalk and
faint cassis. Knows laughter,
but not speech.

A quiet ceorl near town
of Rexford. Buck, and then deer.
A little music of the spheres.

3

Azimuth.
Haruspex. Night mails.
Solstice words with

solstice water cold
and fast. Pale sun on
blond cliffs. A faint breeze

in the old swallow dens. A man
mounts a mare. And the roughlegs,
maculate riders, imperial

boreal tilt
and tack, wiser than owls,
drift disdainfully south.

4

The last magpies I'll see
for several days. Bright cassis
eyes. That yesterday was

solstice eve turned me
in my sleep—that the known world
winters at its ease

with royal goldeneyes
dead center. (Pliny saw
a dead centaur, carried

from Arabia to Rome—
preserved in honey!
"Fierce face. Hairy arms.")

Thin shelves of ice
below the bridge. Half
a handful on the brow

just east from New Almelo.
Old bobbers and line
caught in its limbs—

the tree "fishes."
Carmen misses sunshine, Olga
misses wind. Leave these

snowflakes all down the valley
staking claim to hold
these streams from further folly.

As they were saying
in the north: "Ears. Bad straps.
Heron impersonator called in

to pick up the worms beaten
from the hide. Raven/swan/raven/
swan/raven. Jumping around,

jumping around over everything
even the holy things . . ."
Which ears? Stars

lives like geese across a moon.
Some in honey. Left the rest
in an oriole nest.

Down near Cedar, a day
for a feast: one egg
from a hen

coddled on a thin
candle, to be cracked
and salted on a

Solomon beach
down toward the town
of Cedar

as the hawks go over.
Firmer fare tonight,
on east, with friends.

Blond cliffs.
In an ancient world like this
is, the penalty for harming

a live tree—navel cut out,
spiked to the injured trunk
then driven around

and around it
till full length
of the gut is wrapped

about the tree.
A sort of May Day
upside down.

An old tune, "The Lights of Crow":
Just a hint of solstice hand
for solstice hill, the hills between

the rivers, dark starless night,
Tongue River to the Greasy Grass.
A little push for the cold Divide,

midnight snow. (We carry oranges
and a little glass.)
Over the hump and through

black pines—
                    Just till we see
the lights of Crow.

Greta misses glaciers. Rita
misses rain. And they were saying
in the south: "Far Off.

Hands in Air. Sucks Quick.
Picks It Up and Packs It. Maggots
All Over the Thing.

Questioned Hard Because of That Ring."
They rig an auger on the heights.
In the stream a swirl of cress,

the first true green since yesterday
back west. Washed blue. And don't forget
Mr. Walter Mitty in your solstice dream.

11

They gather wood/
the faint cassis as if
to make a fire

but cannot get it
going. Little larks
struck down cold

along the road, spirits
flown. Swan/raven/swan/
raven/swan.

A plume of smoke
ten miles south, straight
as string, as plumb.

Hawks all distant day
ring the fraction hours:
Moth-chiefs and red tails

at large: Forty in a hundred miles.
The audience, the ear intended
(understood), always the elms,

the goldeneyes dead center.
I say elms because I talk of cottonwoods
incessantly

but I mean cottonwoods all day
and goldeneyes dead center.

Winter star rests/in the oriole nest.

AUGUST BOY

MERRILL W. J. TRAPHAGAN
BORN AUGUST 1, 2004

Wood nymphs come down
the canyons, the word *ocelli*
follows, then swallowtails,

maybe a Leopardspot
or the White Peacock. Even
a Painted Lady—make it

a Painted Lady,
Painted Lady on the outside,
Kodiak Quaker and Smoky Buckeye

on the rail, Creole,
Blue Wave, Checkerspot farther
back, Calico and Dagger Tail

bringing up the rear. It's Creole
and Painted Lady, Creole, Creole,
Painted Lady . . . Blue Wave

makes a move . . . But it's Creole,
no, it's Painted Lady,
Painted Lady by a hairstreak!

All heading your way.

SOMETHING FOR JOHN CLARE

Spiderwort, the begs-
to-be-said: Fat of the summer,
off at the crack of the fat
of the bat. A pair of grosbeaks
feed in a hackberry tree
so lost in it all they have
a sort of kundalini air.
Orioles prefer the goatsbeard.
We watch the slow horses trail
the way Baudelaire, a Frenchman
who followed you through,
watched the clouds: a file
of chestnuts and flashy bays plod
across a meadow, drift?
it seems like hours, head to tail
past a clutter of fallen cottonwoods,
disappear up a cool box elder draw.
Then we watch the clouds.

PLENUM FROM A NUMBER OF PLACES

1

Midday mid-Atlantic,
　　　Heathrow to Newark,
lowbrow December sun booms
　　　through leftside windows.

So-and-so
　　　　　appears on screen—
everyone laughs.
　　　　　So-and-so enters—everyone
sighs. Somebody sings—
　　　everyone cries.
83, 22, 61 percent.
　　　　16, 79, 37.

Dreamt cheese
        ("Piles of riches").
Sea lanes—
    started to write
sea streets—
        glisten.

2

In Paris a cardinal,
      coq de Virginie,
was the Condé's cup
      of tea:
"I'll have one of those"—
      and across the sea
a red bird went,
      singing on deck,
sleeping in the hold.
      Then a lacquered
coach ride up the Seine.

        At Etowah,
Etowah,
  the red oak leaves float
one by one,
    layering the moat
and the mockingbird
      on the flagpole
seen today as
  smoky-granite bystander
secessionist gray.

Siksika boy
    up on the Bow
spells it
    of course
with Victorian *e*,
      g-r-e-y,
and off beyond that
    a gorgeous Georgic kidney pie.

3

Mid-Septembers
     the chiles come up,
Call to Feast:
     Caballo, Socorro,
Alamillo: a steady stream
     up Rio Bravo—
a lot like Lincoln's casket
     through the East.

Dreamt snow
     (piles of cheese)
cool in the head.
     Mars red.
Mountains with their sometime
     baddog hooligan look
to the west.

     Each night
the little ink monkey creeps
from the cupboard,
     sharpens
the pencils, straightens
     the desk, the faces.

Cream teal
    jump wild, know sting
of shot:
  "lucky to be alive"—

  True in All Places.

MORNING WITH CHOKECHERRIES

Douse them, wet
they shine like brilliant
caviar (dust devils whirling,
cranes circling, babies
laughing, halfmoon sailing,
ravens, old station wagons
circling and circling), set
them in the sun.

PARAPH

Picking up a cup
of coffee, picking up
the image: sugar and cream,
my first, age seven or eight:
My mother made it for me:
It must have been an Irish way.

And O the Irish had it bad,
boys, don't get me started on that—
Brian's mom at Niagara
refused to cross to Canada, wouldn't
set foot, that's how bad
they had it.

Behold the coffeed coast:

the cream and sugar,
the kittiwake/lacewing beam
of the ligature: (beyond the alley
old man Donnewirth starts his snazzy
Studebaker): the oven on with the door
open to warm us at our toast.

YAMPA CROWS AT YAMPA EVENING

Subject pilfered,
lightly repainted: poetry
as subtlest of craws: crows

at sundown
fine print for omnivores.
They sit on old boxcars—

"Alabama State Docks/
Port of Mobile"—doors
wide open, see right through:

sand bar, willows, Yampa,
alders, foothills, half-lit peaks:
the Williams Fork Range.

☞

Claybank: one,
one of a yellowish color: dun,
ochraceous dun. And Oleg

phoned: new paintings
not quite dry: "Truckers
Diving," scenes at a motel pool

in blistered country, western August,
men with beards and bellies
leaping on the board

or caught in glaring midair
above the aqua water,
coiled wire and cactus off beyond.

☞

Any big moon
bearing a dark V
makes for a *meadowlark*

moon. She
(evening river) brushing
the hair to curry the thoughts.

It (imaginary cecropia number)
"rises from our
bodies, our brains . . ."

Though only an ass
would describe himself
"delectable."

☞

Dennis Dilda's final meal,
Arizona Territory, 1886
(the crime the Bloody Murder):

Fried chicken, broiled chops,
sirloin steak, oysters,
peas, potatoes, bread,

jelly, coffee and cake.
(It tenders
the blackbirds as fruit

of the willow, it renders
the outfielders friendlier
than the in.)

☞

Look to the high country: firn
of the spoken. The storm a crone
deep in the south.

Moon teal speckled
like fat trout. Souls slip around—
eastsiders end up in New Orleans,

westsiders in Chinatown.
Single (type) specimen found hanging
from a rusty coathook near the door

of an aromatic inn. Orange-brown.
Stronger than pheasant, paler, more
yellow than oriole or *feuille mort* . . .

☞

I've been thinking hard
about that early evening drive,
finespun light Broadus

to Belle Fourche,
dismantling a capon, tossing out
bones for coyotes along the way,

happiest of men.
A farmyard gate left open
at a certain angle, the white goat

tied in a coded (say, southeast)
corner of the field, or simply
upstairs westside windows

☞

in an old summer house, sashes
raised in a semaphoric pattern:
"Never said Boo to a goose."

Lilacs after,
as a sort of wake—
It set the pale Romeos

beside the Adelaide Dunbars
and the Longfellows beside
the Montaignes.

It left the Desdemonas
with the General Wm. T. Shermans
and the Edmond Boissiers!

☞

Easy now. Crows
and possible alpenglow.
Gobs of worms drifted

about midnight over the flooded
lawns of riverside cabins.
But that gambling boy in Elko

wanted to share his winnings
with me just because I stood
behind his chair. Bees come down

like deer to sip at the river.
Aligns with three hundred twenty-eight
full-blood Cheyennes in Denver.

☞

Some wines are best
drunk from cupped hands.
Nodding constantly

like ponies in August
chasing flies. Piñon jays
on the far bank

just cracked a piñata.
"I see great peace
coming your way."

My old friend. Big
old grin. Groundhog gravy
all over her chin.

☞

Dun: dun
heightened, raised,
hoisted with sorrel.

The first one
to never say
"Constantinople."

Affable young cottonwood
cools
in late light.

Crows fade. *Joie de*.
Joie de pisser.
The last one to never say "Istanbul."

RUNE: CAMAS PRAIRIE

One Time
           in a roll
of the eyes:
           Appaloosa colts
all ears and legs:
           Last one in's
the rotten egg.

BALLAD CALCAREOUS

Those were long words
in your last letter, tall
pines. We were talking
a skillet of ham—

streamlined—ever since
Faulkner's "Mule in the Yard"
and finally drove up
into the hills

to make a fire, up
to the limestone côtes,
brink high above, summer
below, a tough place

to run out of ink,
and beside the limestone
road a dead dog cried,
saddlesore bitch

with swollen teats,
wanted in five states
for lascivious tricks—
two boys were there

digging a grave
in the limestone bank, leaning
on their spades as we went by:
Dog's Hole: Cynossēma!

Not many Hecubas nowadays
on the girls-school rolls.
Peace to her combustible soul.
We found a cedar and scratched

a match and fried our ham,
fried it high, one gull overhead
like a kite on a line,
and cut back down the hill.

ROSEBUD FAIR

Shrimp-on-a-stick
and Monkey Pie: Berry soup
and marzipans: Blue ribbon rhubarb,
and everyone moving widdershins!

The Calamus this morning—
that was a suckling stream,
off in its hills: first gathering,
summoning: catch of good rain
not far back, and greenness—sweet flag—
for the pilgrim. And now it lingers
as an emblem on the afternoon,
so light on its feet an emblem
in a Heraldry: reach of convocation,
all things forth, abroad, afoot
in its hills: a Soil with Gentians,
if that's what they were: catch
of sweet rain, recently fallen.

Berry soup and marzipan:
Ride the buckskin, ride the Scrambler:
Licorice sticks as long as your arm,
five or six to the dollar!

SIX SONGS

1

In Jane's *World Railways*,
Jane's book of trains,

those days shot past again:
We were camped at Vouvray: Vouvray

cheese in a creel, two bottles
tethered in the Loire. In the cold water

grasses wave. (A Z-2 emu takes a curve
on the outskirts of Fleurville—

in Jane's *World Railways*,
Jane's book of trains.

2

The Huck Finn house,
a utopian lair: sashes sag
in the photo, shingles flare.

A curly-tailed mutt
sniffs something rare
beside the walk.

Solid walnut, a quick
back alley into town.
Someone tinted

the raggy flowers
near the stairs
slapdash mustard-

marigold, the dog
in thought a deep utopian
honey-brindle-brown.

3

Someone from Port Said said,
The yucca is an evergreen—
Tiny goatee like a tuft of baleen.

    And haven't I seen you
    on the Snake River plain?
    Where sage is the sailaway
    and the water looks like rain?

The one from Port Said said,
Those sparrows in the blue flax—
a posse for parallax.

    And don't I know you
    from the Snake River plain?
    Where sage is the sailaway
    and the water tastes like rain?

4

So it was Jocko with you there
at Chaco and the night before?

The spy plane miles above
sees people moving through the ruins
but not the juncoes on the kiva floor.

       To prevent,
       prevent from leaving
       as by speaking

       intently
       to them although
       they are hot for the door.

5

O red bandanna—

(You might be like those men
in Dante pausing from their
purgatory, stepping out
from dross to wipe their brows

and hail the stranger: "And how
is the Umpqua?" "And how goes
the Shinnecock?" "And how
runs the Susquehanna?")

6

Abacus
like castanets
in the hands of a maestro:

click-click:
halfway to equinox—
The redbird sings *O peckerhead day*

SHRIKE MUSIC

H.D. died while we
were high school. High
school belle and high school
harry. Lying around

with the radio on
or shooting pool
in Dingtown. Now I see.
Shrike music

from the top
of a tree: halfhearted
notes in listless
medley. But what

other carnivore
can carry a tune?
or even tries? No hawk
song. No gull lullaby.

No heron croon.
Should I relay this

to *Die Zeit*? (Taut
caged shrikes lining

some adobe/granite
ur-portico stair.)
Faint mumblesong
from a poplar top:

Parlando, even
winsome on February air.
Which brings us
to the Disney prayer—

>Rivers, rise,
>take those killing
>men *méchants*

>off downstream
>and out to sea,
>any sea, and

>down again, some
>sour Sargasso
>evermore. Amen.

AN ARTIST'S LIFE

Or, the Beekeeper Blues:
Beekeeper Blues a la carte.
And when the tanagers return,
central May, three, four
to a tree, they shame
my sunburnt heart.

UNDANCEABLE

Wisha, the women
were singing, the song
carried on the air,

moved and melted
down the valley: a place
in-velvet

like an elk: then
the sparrows new-to-
science picked it up

from the yucca stalks,
the songs in tandem
filled the bottoms

like a day (we knew
in a waking world it was
Tongue River with chicory

and the sparrows were
breweri—but *Thoughts of you*
looked our way.

2

Some days wanting gulls
below. Three roans in the shallows,
one of them blue.

We held to prehistoric routes
still kicking: smoothworn edges
over easy: "Crow Ford"
to the Yellowstone . . .

The pretty lancehead found
among the cactus flowers by one of those
for whom it was originally honed:
That hillside has a sense of humor.

Kingbird gambit, kingbird rules.

3

Dauber swallows build their town
no hands. Two thousand trips
to the mudhole.

"This is where they bring the senators
to fast naked in the muck, wail
for prudence from the sucker fin."

We meant to stop and paint
the old hotels fronting the tracks
in Poplar, get the distant river trees
reflected in the dusty glass,

but it was Thursday, and we
were Sunday painters, by then
we were facing the Killdeer range—

And everywhere the million sunflowers
gazing.

4

That was Old Woman Creek
caught your eye, the staggered
falling fifths a surprise
distaff in the basso.
A rough night, compañero.
One spotty fawn dead
on the centerstripe, several
nighthawks also down.
Then we were behind a man
in a daffodil Olds whose ears
stuck out in silhouette against
the plains, way out, just like
a lad I knew in school
days. He could touch his tongue
to the tip of his nose
no hands. Mimicked ominous
distant thunder from the back
of the study halls. We envied his
idiolect and his rumpled look.
Some of us suspected he had
connections with the Kinsey book.
Could it be? Way out on Old Woman Creek?
We followed him in duple time
from Red Bird to Jay Em.

5

Since you asked:
It is a pomander:
But this is not a moral tract.

Please find enclosed:
one sun-dried male yellow-head
from the berm of the Mahto road.

6

You know those breaks west
from Cut Meat . . .
                              ! Take it all
by night, run it by moonlight
and moonlight only

for a week, Moonshell valley
and the Moreau with the top down
four a.m., sidereal bareback, miles

of Sandhills by lightning strike
white as day, Taurus
and the little Sisters, three roans

pure chiaroscuro, lunar buttes
and night sage in the head,
locking down at daybreak, blinds

drawn tight, then out again
with poor-wills at darkfall,
Sweetgrass Hills, the Bear Paws

whose Milky Way—

7

Further instigations

        from Ancient Wisdoms

transcribed in the form

        of a waltz.

SMOKE TODAY

To the west
just off that lightning-rod
ridge, a lazy gray
smoke curl, a simple up

and out, left
to right. Burning off
the tumbleweeds, burning off
piranha ticks.

It makes me long
for a Lucky Strike.

Early today, far above
faroff Prairie Dog Creek,
a miles-long ribbon

flowed elegantly east,
undulant fretless umber

almost not quite really there—
burning off the buckaroo

wallpaper. It made me dream
of a Gauloise blue.

SALAL

1

Dark waters
at the foot of the mountain:
Salal: Salal muckamuck

(to wet a finger
in the pidgin wind).
We sleep arm in arm

beneath clement Pendletons,
wake to find pines
between people on the south

lagoon. The great Dane wrote the Sea
is simply often
the first to say *No*—stars

soon to follow. Breakers
exPLODE, the running
of the gulls, aiheee.

2

Shag. Shell.
"Boy Cleaning Fish."
Geishas once whitened
their faces with powdered
droppings of the nightingale.
But then beyond, half a mile
out, through the glasses we pick up
scoters, there beyond the surf
and surge, hundreds in an open
flock, the main corps, true scoter,
riding swells, all facing
north: cordon and cortex
of the kind, in speciality:
and that they tear off
mussels to swallow them whole
and the gizzards grind them
Beowulfian
to the brilliant obsidian/
purple sand we find in
wandering driftlines on the beach—
called *scoter dust* or '
scoter meal, aiheee.

3

I heard your horse
this morning
calling Opus 17.

Muddy boys gut
hapless ling.
Heartwood

in sumptuary stanzas
far-to-sea. At dawn
the first headlights

around the 101 bend,
northbound, sweep
the mysteries: clean

hills close together,
cowrie smile. Thin
red ink squeezed

from blue salal.
And poetry will surely
win—what could stand up

to such a force
pounding the shores
nightlong day

after day? aiheee.

☞

NOTES & ACKNOWLEDGMENTS

The Solomon River rises near the 101st meridian and runs easterly across the high plains of far northwestern Kansas. The Yampa flows through western Colorado. Cynossēma ("Ballad Calcareous"): "Dog's hole," the name for the burial place of Hecuba, devastated queen of Troy, after she was metamorphosed into a bitch. Rosebud Fair: an annual late-summer gathering on the Rosebud Sioux reservation, South Dakota. Moonshell River ("Undanceable"): an old native name for the North Platte River. Salal: an abundant, blue-berried shrub of the Oregon coast; "the great Dane" is, of course, Isak Dinesen.

"Yampa Crows at Yampa Evening" appeared in *Sal Mimeo* and "Six Songs" in *Chicago Review*.

MERRILL GILFILLAN

was born in Mount Gilead, Ohio, and studied literature at the Universities of Michigan and Iowa. His first book of poems appeared in 1970. Recent publications include two books of poetry, *The Seasons* (2002) and *Small Weathers* (2004), as well as a collection of al fresco essays, *Rivers and Birds* (2003). He currently lives in Colorado.